Ribbons!

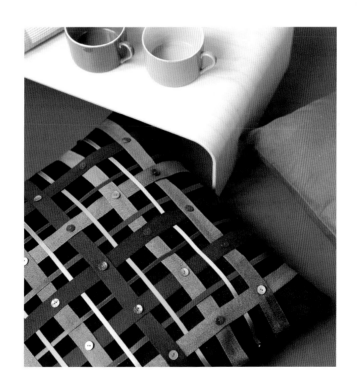

D&C
David and Charles

Suppliers

UK

The Rocking Rabbit Trading Co,
7 The Green,
Haddenham, CB6 3TA, UK
Tel: 0870 606 1588
www.rockingrabbit.co.uk

Fred Aldous,
37 Lever Street,
Manchester, M1 1LW, UK
Tel: 0870 751 7301
www.fredaldous.co.uk

Crafty Ribbons,
3 Beechwood Clump Farm,
Tin Pot Lane,
Blandford, DT11 7TD, UK
Tel: 01258 455889
www.craftyribbons.com

Regalcrafts,
269 Meadow Way,
Leighton Buzzard, LU7 3XS, UK
www.regalcrafts.com

The Ribbon Company,
PO Box 1114,
Aldbury, HP23 5WS, UK
Tel: 07875 429808
www.ribbonmoon.co.uk

The Home Counties Wholesale Ltd,
Unit C 6 Honours,
Tring, HP23 6AF, UK
Tel: 01442 891183
www.wholesales.co.uk

USA

As Cute as a Button,
Canon St, Ste G,
San Diego, CA92106, USA
Tel: 619 223 2555
www.ascuteasabutton.com

Brightlings Beads,
107 Milley Brook Court,
Cary, NC27519, USA
Tel: 919 388 9822
www.brightlingsbeads.com

Thread Art,
16433 Mueschke Road, Ste B,
Cypress, TX77433, USA
Tel: 281 373 5058
www.threadart.com

JKM Products,
431 Commerce Lane, Ste B,
West Berlin, NJ08091, USA
Tel: 856 767 6604
www.jkmribbon.com

Vogue Fabrics,
623-27 W Roosevelt Rd,
Chicago, IL60607, USA
Tel: 312 829 2505
www.voguefabricstore.com

A DAVID & CHARLES BOOK

© Dessain et Tolra/Larousse 2005
Originally published in France as *Fantaisies de rubans*

David & Charles is an F+W Publications Inc. company
4700 East Galbraith Road
Cincinnati, OH 45236

First published in the UK in 2007

A catalogue record for this book is available from the British Library.

ISBN-13: 978-0-7153-2841-5 paperback
ISBN-10: 0-7153-2841-7 paperback

Printed in China by SNP Leefung Pte Ltd
for David & Charles
Brunel House   Newton Abbot   Devon

Visit our website at www.davidandcharles.co.uk

David & Charles books are available from all good bookshops; alternatively you can contact our Orderline on 0870 9908222 or write to us at FREEPOST EX2 110, D&C Direct, Newton Abbot, TQ12 4ZZ (no stamp required UK only); US customers call 800-289-0963 and Canadian customers call 800-840-5220.

Layout: P.A.C. studio@pakenko.com
Photography: Cactus Studio – Fabrice Besse
photographs on p.10 and p.19 (technical photos): Olivier Ploton
Illustrations: Lucie Niney
Photoengraving: Arts Graphiques du Centre

Contents

Key to symbols

★

Easy

★★

Of moderate
difficulty

★★★

Complicated

FOREWORD

We have all gone into a haberdashery or fabric store and longingly touched the satin-smooth ribbons in a myriad of colours lining the shelves. Ribbons have it all: they come in a multitude of colours, materials and textures, offering an unparalleled choice and allowing the crafter free rein to play with transparencies, pleats, gathers and shiny effects. Not forgetting braids and cords, which have hundreds of other uses besides curtain tiebacks!

And this is precisely the aim of this book. It will show you how to embellish, make over, customize, create, jazz up and completely transform your clothes, accessories and even household objects with just a few strips of fabric. Satin, silk, cotton, suede, organza, velvet, cord, grosgrain, ric-rac, edged and waxed ribbon – the choice is huge! And why not make your own ribbons from linen, canvas or any other fabric you like?

Once you have your ribbons, the world is your oyster. You can stick on, wind, glue, sew, fringe, tear, gather, fold and – most importantly – have fun letting your imagination run wild as you develop your own style, customize your clothes and enhance your home. The possibilities are endless: you could use ribbons as the main feature in your designs, or as that finishing touch that, when added to a piece of material or a frame, will set your item apart. You can also combine ribbons with other fabrics, beads, sequins and buttons for sophisticated and original designs.

Grab your scissors!

BASIC EQUIPMENT

1. DMC stranded cotton
2. Sewing thread
3. Pins
4. Dressmaker's pencil
5. Chenille needles, fine needles and thimble
6. Embroidery scissors
7. Tape measure
8. Rocaille beads and round beads
9. Novelty sequins
10. Coloured shell buttons
11. Sequins
12. Cabochons
13. Sequin tape
14. Wooden skewers

BASIC EQUIPMENT

1. Craft mesh
2. Ribbon and braid fabric glue
3. Small foam roller
4. Eyelet punch, punching tips, setting tips, eyelets
5. Iron-on fabric
6. Dressmaker's scissors
7. Coloured inks
8. Metal ruler

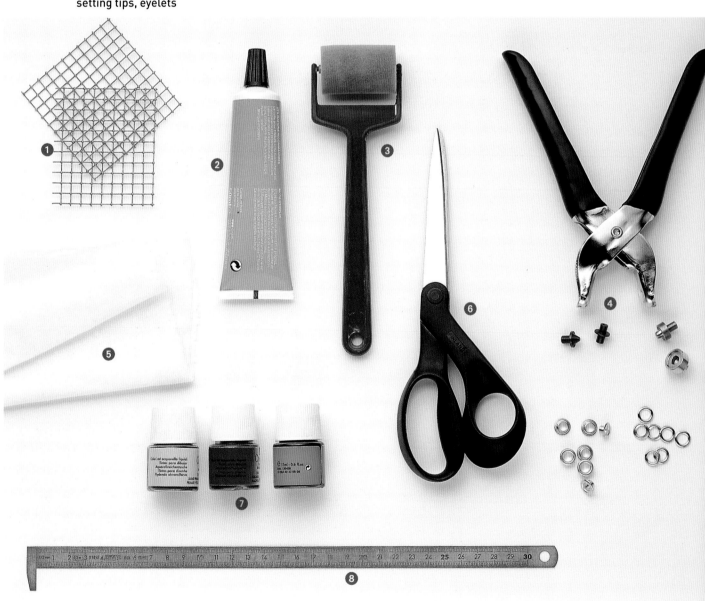

STITCHES

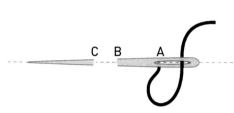

RUNNING STITCH

The most basic of all the stitches. Insert the needle in and out along a line in front of you and pull the thread through, keeping the lengths of your stitches uniform. Bring the needle out at A, down through B, then up again at C. Pull the thread through and begin the sequence again.

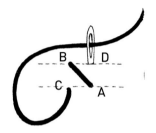

CROSS STITCH

Bring the needle out at A, go into B and come out again at C. To complete the stitch, go back through D.

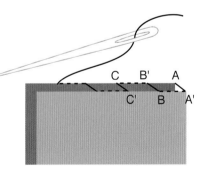

LADDER STITCH

This stitch is used principally for joining together two pieces of fabric with concealed stitching. Insert your needle into A, then into A'. Pass the needle through the fold in the front piece of fabric. Come out at B and into B', and repeat.

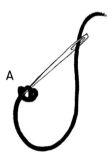

FRENCH KNOT

1 Bring your needle out at A and loop the thread two or three times around the needle from right to left.
2 Bring the loops together, then slide them to the end of the needle. Go back through your fabric close to A and pull the thread from the back of the fabric to make the knot.

RIBBONS

1. Silk ribbon
2. Satin ribbon
3. Patterned ribbon
4. Edged polyester ribbon
5. Pleated satin ribbon
6. Velvet ribbon
7. Gingham ribbon
8. Gathered ribbon
9. Corporate branded ribbon
10. Sheer ribbon
11. Grosgrain
12. Cotton ribbon
13. Elasticated gathered ribbon
14. Chiffon ribbon
15. Suede ribbon
16. Lace ribbon

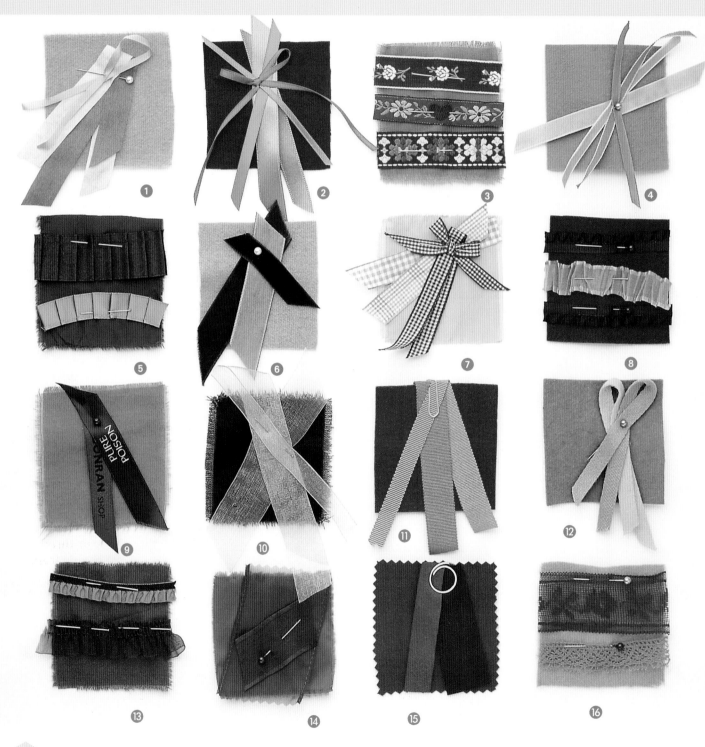

CORDS AND BRAIDS

1. Fine cord
2. Braid and fringing
3. Flower braid
4. Ric-rac braid
5. Waxed cotton cord
6. Rat-tail cord
7. Braid and strapping
8. Cord
9. Piping and soutache braid

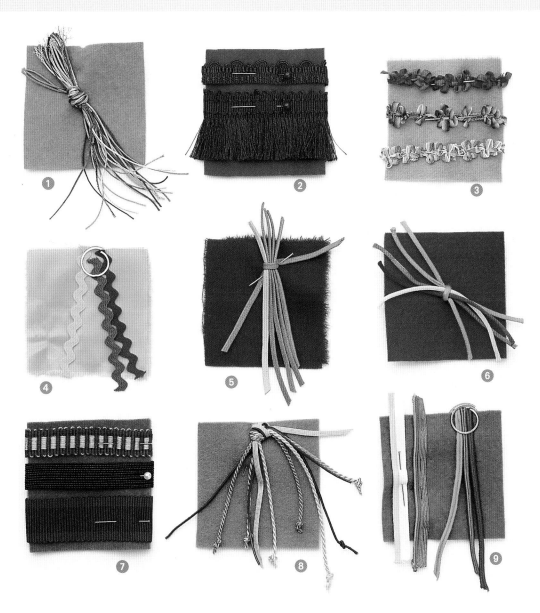

CARE INSTRUCTIONS
Clothes and accessories decorated with ribbons should be washed inside out (by hand or in a special bag in the machine for very delicate designs) and ironed on the reverse. Items decorated with braid and cord, velvet ribbons and three-dimensional designs should be dry-cleaned.

SATIN BEADS★★

Strips of satin ribbon make perfect beads
for shimmering jewellery and accessories.

MATERIALS REQUIRED **NECKLACE**

1m (40in) satin ribbon 1cm (½in) wide in dark pink, light pink, orange, plum and orange-pink

1m (40in) satin ribbon 5mm (¼in) wide in red

Wooden skewer

Ribbon fabric glue

Chenille needle and pins

DMC stranded cotton in red, pink and orange

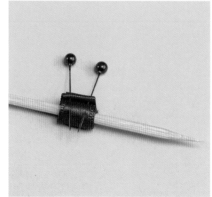

1 To make each bead, cut a 15cm (6in) length of ribbon, fold in half and wrap it around a skewer, starting from the two cut ends of the ribbon. Apply a little glue to the ribbon on the first loop to secure.

2 Wrap the rest of your ribbon tightly around the skewer and secure with pins. Cut a 10cm (4in) length of DMC stranded cotton, wrap it around the bead and tie a very tight double knot. Take out the pins and slide the bead off the skewer.

3 Make up around 20 beads in this way, using contrasting colours for your ribbons and the DMC stranded cotton. Using a chenille needle, thread the beads on to the 5mm (¼in) red satin ribbon.

BRACELET ★ ★ ★

MATERIALS REQUIRED

1.5m (60in) satin ribbon 1.5cm (¾in) wide in khaki, celadon green and turquoise

DMC stranded cotton in green and turquoise

1 spool elasticated thread in green

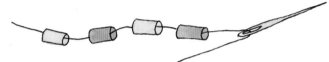

1 Make up your beads by following the instructions for the necklace on page 10, alternating between the three colours as you go. Make up enough beads to fit your wrist when placed side by side.

2 Cut a 1.5m (60in) length of elasticated thread and thread on your beads, alternating the colours as you go. Leave 5cm (2in) excess elastic at each end to tie your bracelet together.

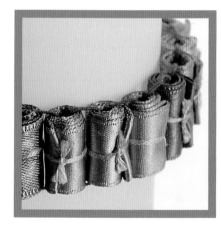

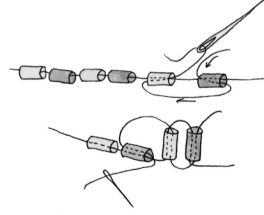

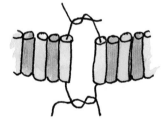

3 Cut a 2m (80in) length of elasticated thread and thread it through the tops of the beads so they sit side by side. Using the two diagrams as a guide, line the beads up as you work.

4 Bring the two ends together and tie a double knot in each length of elasticated thread, using the diagram as a guide.

HAIRSLIDE ★ ★ ★

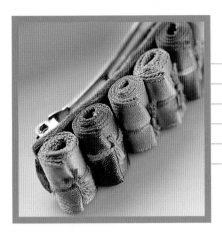

MATERIALS REQUIRED

1m (40in) satin ribbon 1.5cm (¾in) wide in pink, celadon green and turquoise

DMC stranded cotton in pink and turquoise

1 hairslide 8cm (3¼in) long

Ribbon fabric glue

Jewellery glue

Pink felt

① Cut a strip of pink felt to fit the length and width of your hairslide.

② Following the instructions for the necklace on page 10, make up three ribbon beads in each colour. You will need about nine beads for an 8cm (3¼in) hairslide.

③ Use fabric glue to stick the beads side by side on to the strip of felt, alternating the colours as you go. Leave to dry, then glue the design on to your hairslide with jewellery glue.

PARTY BAG ★★

A small tote bag made from wild silk and decorated with ribbons. Very haute couture!

MATERIALS REQUIRED

1m (40in) silk fabric 140cm (55in) wide in pink

1m (40in) gathered ribbon in dark pink

1m (40in) grosgrain 1cm (½in) wide in orange

1m (40in) grosgrain 1cm (½in) wide in dark pink

1m (40in) large ric-rac braid

1m (40in) satin ribbon 1cm (½in) wide in pink

1m (40in) pleated ribbon 1cm (½in) wide

1m (40in) edged silk ribbon 1cm (½in) wide

1m (40in) cotton ribbon 1cm (½in) wide in pink

1m (40in) edged satin ribbon 1cm (½in) wide

1m (40in) tubular ribbon for the handles

Pink thread

Dressmaker's pencil

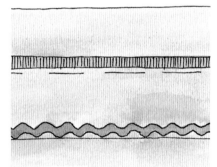

1 Cut a strip of pink silk 32cm (12½in) wide and 1m (40in) long. Mark a horizontal line with the dressmaker's pencil 4cm (1⅝in) from one of the short ends. Pin the orange grosgrain ribbon to this line. Using the picture above as a guide, fold 5mm (¼in) of silk up over the ribbon all the way along so that half of the ribbon is hidden. Pin and tack.

2 Using the diagram as a guide, draw a horizontal line 3cm (1¼in) from the previous fold and pin on the ric-rac. Make a fold in the same way as before, covering the edge of the ric-rac, pin and tack. Repeat for all the types of ribbon.

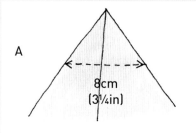

A

8cm
(3¼in)

B

③ When you have added the last ribbon, leave a gap of 13cm (5¼in), then add the same ribbons to the other side of the bag, the opposite way up. Continue working in this way towards the top of the bag, making each fold 2cm (⅞in) from the upper edge of the previous ribbon and adding the ribbons in the same order.

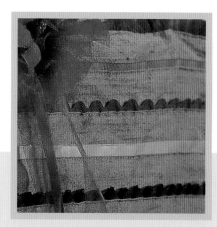

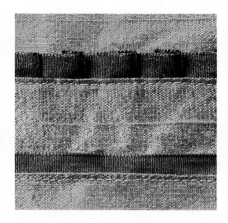

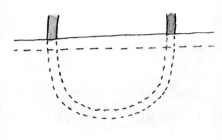

C

4 When all the ribbons are tacked in place, machine-stitch 2mm ($^2/_{32}$in) from the edge of each fold in pink thread. Fold the bag in half, right sides together, so that the ribbons match up and trim off any excess fabric. Next, sew up the sides. To make the base of the bag, make an 8cm (3¼in) triangle at each corner, using diagrams A and B opposite as a guide. Machine-stitch across.

5 Cut out a strip of silk the same size as your bag for the lining. Right sides facing, sew the edges together, leaving an 8cm (3¼in) opening on one side. Stitch the triangles that will make the base of your lining. Pin the gathered ribbon to the top edge of the bag so that the gathers lie downwards. When the lining has been attached and turned through the ribbon will stand up round the edge as shown above. Stuff the bag into the lining, right sides together, sandwiching the gathered ribbon.

6 To attach the handles, cut two 39cm (15½in) lengths of tubular ribbon. Using diagram C as a guide, place the handles between the bag and the lining, then stitch 1cm (½in) from the edge all the way around the top. Turn the bag out through the gap in the lining and topstitch on the right side 2mm ($^2/_{32}$in) from the upper edge. Sew up the gap in the lining with ladder stitch (see page 7).

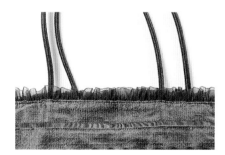

FRINGE JEWELLERY ★★

A splash of colour and originality to complement your outfit.

MATERIALS REQUIRED **BRACELET**

16cm (6½in) sheer ribbon 4cm (1⅝in) wide in dark pink

16cm (6½in) sheer ribbon 4cm (1⅝in) wide in pink

16cm (6½in) sheer ribbon 2cm (⅞in) wide in plum

30cm (12in) satin ribbon 5mm (¼in) wide in shocking pink

Small faceted sequins in pink

Small round beads

Pins

Pink thread

Fine needle

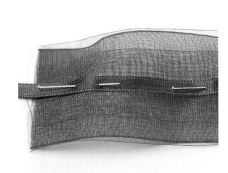

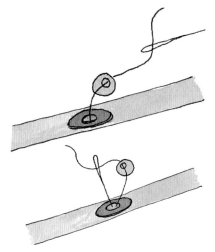

❶ Assemble your ribbons. Place the two widest ribbons one on top of the other. Next, place the sheer plum ribbon in the centre and the thin satin ribbon on top, leaving lengths of satin ribbon at each end for ties. Pin to secure and then tack the four ribbons together.

❷ Using the diagram as a guide, sew the sequins and beads on to the satin ribbon 3mm (⅛in) apart. Take out the tacking.

❸ Cut 5mm (¼in) wide fringes in the three sheer ribbons. Tie the bracelet using the satin ribbon.

MATERIALS REQUIRED **LARGE FLOWER**

20cm (8in) sheer ribbon 4cm (1⅝in) wide in dark pink

20cm (8in) sheer ribbon 4cm (1⅝in) wide in light pink

20cm (8in) sheer ribbon 2cm (⅞in) wide in plum

50cm (19¾in) satin ribbon 5mm (¼in) wide in shocking pink

1 felt disc 5mm (¼in) in diameter in pink or purple

Small faceted sequins and round beads in pink

Ribbon fabric glue and a safety pin

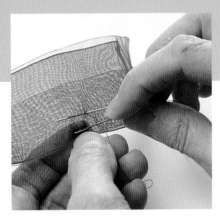

❶ Place your 4cm (1⅝in) wide ribbons and the 2cm (⅞in) wide plum ribbon one on top of the other. Pin together and sew a small running stitch (see page 7) 3mm (⅛in) from the edge of the ribbons. Cut 5mm (¼in) wide fringes along the length of the ribbons.

❷ Pull gently on the thread to gather the ribbons evenly. Tie in a circle to make a flower.

❸ Carefully glue the felt disc to the back of the flower, placing your satin ribbon folded in half between the flower and the felt leaving a loop one side and the two ends on the other. Sew a safety pin to the felt disc.

Make the smaller flower using the same technique. Use two lengths of purple ribbon 2cm (⅞in) wide, one on top of the other. Secure the flower on a satin ribbon 3mm (⅛in) wide with a sequin and a bead.

❹ Decorate the centre of the flower with five sequins and beads sewn on in a circle, using step 2 on page 18 as a guide.

SUEDE RIBBON FLOWERS★★

MATERIALS REQUIRED **CHOKER**

50cm (19¾in) suede ribbon 7cm (2¾in) wide in pink

20cm (8in) sheer ribbon 7cm (2¾in) wide in pink

1 sequin and 1 pink bead

Safety pin

1 Cut a 20cm (8in) strip of suede 6.5cm (2½in) wide and a 50cm (19¾in) strip 5mm (¼in) wide. Use the remaining suede to cut out two discs, one 2cm (⅞in) in diameter and the other 1.5cm (¾in) in diameter.

2 Place your wide suede ribbon and sheer ribbon one on top of the other, matching one edge, and sew together following the instructions for the large flower opposite.

3 To make the centre of the flower, place the 1.5cm (¾in) suede disc, sequin and bead on top, using step 2 on page 18. Glue the other suede disc to the back over the folded narrow strip of suede as in step 3 on page 20. Sew on a safety pin.

A second flower, made entirely from suede, uses the same technique. This time the centre is made of two suede discs placed one on top of the other with a large bead sewn into the middle.

RAG RUG BAG ★★★

Take a simple string bag, some torn-up and knotted silk ribbons and what do you have?
Your own designer bag!

MATERIALS REQUIRED

1 red string bag

1m (40in) pongee silk in vivid red

1m (40in) pongee silk in dark red

1m (40in) satin lining in pink

Red thread

Needle

❶ Lay the string bag out flat on a table and cut across it 25cm (10in) from the opening.

❷ Tear strips of ribbon 5cm (2in) wide from the vivid red and dark red silk. Cut the strips into 20cm (8in) lengths with the ends at a slight angle. Secure the two cut edges of the string bag by knotting a row of ribbons along the bottom.

❸ Cover the bag with knotted ribbons, each two holes apart from the next. Alternate between vivid and dark red ribbons, using more of the vivid red strips.

TOP EDGE OF BAG

6.5cm (2⅝in)

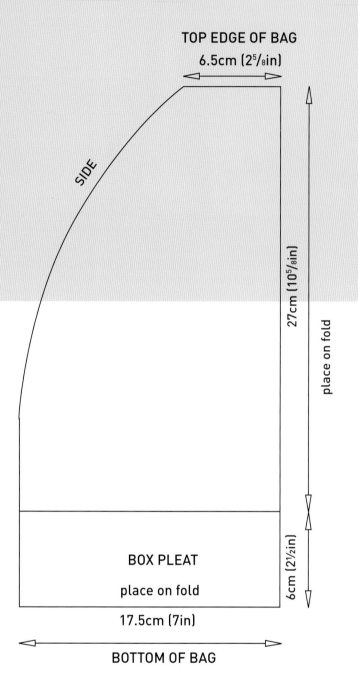

SIDE

27cm (10⅝in)

place on fold

BOX PLEAT

place on fold

6cm (2½in)

17.5cm (7in)

BOTTOM OF BAG

5 Make a box pleat in the bottom of the bag lining to add some give. Sew the lining all the way around with pink thread. Secure the bag by sewing 12cm (4¾in) along each side.

4 Using the diagram as a guide, make a template for the lining. Fold the pink satin into four and cut out the lining. Open the bag out flat and pin the lining on, folding 1.5cm (¾in) on to the reverse. Along the two top edges, allow the lining to overlap the string bag by 2cm (⅞in) so it is visible from the outside, then fold the excess on to the reverse.

FLOWER BELT ★★

MATERIALS REQUIRED

25cm (10in) pongee silk in red

2m (80in) satin ribbon 3mm (¹/₈in) wide in red

1.5m (60in) satin ribbons 5mm (¼in) wide in red and maroon

25cm (10in) red cord

1.5m (60in) velvet ribbon 1cm (½in) wide in red

Red thread

Needle

① Tear your red silk into 5cm (2in) wide strips, then cut into 15cm (6in) lengths with the ends cut at a slight angle. Knot about ten of these ribbons tightly along your cord.

② Make the flower by winding up the cord with the knotted ribbons and securing the roll with a couple of stitches on the underside of the flower. Leave a hole in the middle for the centre of the flower.

③ To make the centre, wind the narrow satin ribbon around three fingers to make a small roll, and place this in the centre of your flower. Secure with a few stitches on the back of the flower.

④ To make the belt, sew the flower on to the end of the three satin and velvet ribbons with a couple of stitches on the back. Tie the belt in a simple knot behind the flower.

FABRIC SHOPPING BAG ★★

A simple design that is easy to make up.
Customize with the flowers of your choice.

MATERIALS REQUIRED

1 small fabric shopping bag

50cm (19¾in) flower print fabric

2m (80in) gingham ribbon 1cm (½in) wide in red

20cm (8in) lengths of the following: gingham ribbon 4cm (1⅝in) wide in red, sequin tape in iridescent orange, narrow ric-rac braid in red and turquoise blue, large ric-rac braid in red, flower ribbon 2cm (⅞in) wide, red grosgrain 1cm (½in) wide, soutache braid 3mm (⅛in) wide in yellow

50cm (19¾in) flower braid in orange and pink

1 red button

6 novelty sequins

50cm (19¾in) thin piping in red

Red thread

Fine needle

① Cut a 17cm (6¾in) square from the flower print fabric. Adapt the size of this square to fit your chosen bag, adding 1cm (½in) all the way around for the hems. Lay your ribbons on the fabric and pin them on, leaving 1cm (½in) excess at each end. Pin a length of red piping to the top of the pocket. Sew the ribbons and piping on to the fabric with a running stitch (see page 7) using red thread.

② Measure round the opening of the bag with a tape measure and cut a strip of the same length plus 2cm (⅞in) and 10cm (4in) wide from the printed fabric. Fold in 1cm (½in) at each end and then fold the strip into three, lengthways. Pin to secure and pin the strip inside the opening of the bag, leaving 1cm (½in) showing at the top. Pin the ric-rac braid 2cm (⅞in) down from the top round the outside of the bag. Machine-stitch the strip together with the ric-rac braid.

③ Place the square pocket on to the bag 6.5cm (2⅝in) below the opening. Pin on the three sides, tucking in 1cm (½in) fabric and the ends of the ribbons. Insert the red piping between the bag and the pocket and secure with a running stitch.

④ Fold an 8cm (3¼in) length of yellow soutache braid in half and sew on in the centre of the top of the pocket. Sew on a button as a closure.

⑤ To finish: pin the gingham ribbon to the handles and sew with a running stitch. Add the flower ribbon either side of the pocket, the large red ric-rac braid across the bottom of the bag, and the narrow turquoise blue ric-rac braid above the pocket. Decorate with novelty sequins.

CUSTOMIZED JEANS ★★

Breathe new life into an old pair of jeans
with colourful flowers and braids.

MATERIALS REQUIRED

1m (40in) red and pink flower ribbon

20cm (8in) sheer gathered ribbon in maroon

1.5m (60in) pleated satin ribbon 2.5cm (1in) wide in vivid red

1.5m (60in) braid 1cm (½in) wide in maroon

15cm (6in) ric-rac braid in vivid red

3m (120in) thin twisted cord in vivid red

3 cabochons (2 red, 1 pink)

White dressmaker's pencil

Red thread

Fine needle

Tracing paper

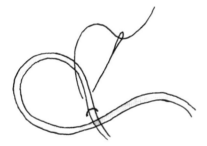

① Lay your jeans out flat. Make a copy of the flower templates on page 64 and transfer them on to your jeans, 4cm (1⅝in) under the right pocket and down the outer seam. Go over the outline with the dressmaker's white pencil. Cut a 50cm (19¾in) length of red cord. Starting at the centre of the flower, make a figure of eight and secure the cord with a simple couching stitch over the top (see diagram). Make a second figure of eight, at right angles to the first, then make the stem by following your pencil outline, and secure using the same technique. Finish each flower by tying a small knot in the end of the cord. Sew on a cabochon at the centre of the flower.

② Lay the pleated ribbon and braid one on top of the other over the right pocket, leaving 1cm (½in) excess at each end which is folded over to the inside. Attach with a running stitch (see page 7). Do the same round the bottom of the jeans, starting from the inner seam of each leg. On the second pocket, lay the gathered ribbon and ric-rac on top of each other, leaving 1cm (½in) excess at each end which is folded over to the inside. Secure with a running stitch.

③ Place the flower ribbon along the bottom of the waistband and secure with a running stitch.

PARTY TOPS★

Feathers and beads for special occasions.

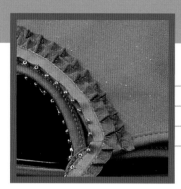

MATERIALS REQUIRED

RED CAMISOLE TOP

1.5m (60in) gathered ribbon 1cm (½in) wide in maroon

Rocaille beads in iridescent red

Threads to match

Fine needle

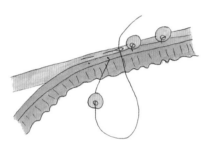

Starting from the back of the camisole, place the gathered ribbon along the first strap, then across the front. Continue along the second strap, then across the back. Using the diagram as a guide, secure the ribbon with ladder stitch (see page 7), threading on one bead every 1cm (½in). To prevent puckering, do not pin the ribbon before sewing and do not pull on the thread too tightly. Cut a second length of ribbon for the second row on the front of the top.

Leave 1cm (½in) excess at each end to fold over on to the back of the top. Slide the second ribbon under the first and sew with a running stitch (see page 7).

MATERIALS REQUIRED

BLACK LONG-SLEEVED T-SHIRT

1.5m (60in) black feather ribbon

2m (80in) satin ribbon 1cm (½in) wide in black

Black thread

Needle

Measure around the neckline of the T-shirt and cut a length of feather ribbon 2cm (⁷/₈in) longer. Do the same for the cuffs. Starting at the front in the centre, sew the ribbon around the neckline with stitches every 5cm (2in). Knot the thread every time and pull it through gently so as to keep the elasticity of the fabric. Do the same at the sleeves. Tie a bow in the satin ribbon and stitch to the centre of the neckline.

CLUTCH BAG AND BELT★★

Ribbons are teamed with felt
in these trendy and original matching accessories.

MATERIALS REQUIRED **CLUTCH BAG**

42 x 32cm (16½ x 12½in) rectangle of red wool felt

Branded ribbons

DMC stranded cotton in green, yellow, orange, turquoise, purple, red, blue and pink

Needle

Orange thread

Dressmaker's pencil

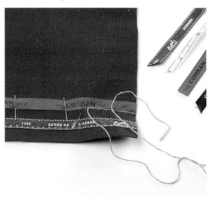 

① Cut one rectangle 21 x 32cm (8¼ x 12½in) and two rectangles 21 x 15.5cm (8¼ x 6¼in) in red felt. Cut 23cm (9in) lengths of ribbon. Make a mark 1cm (½in) from the lower edge of the large rectangle with a dressmaker's pencil and pin on the first ribbon, folding the ends to the reverse. Sew it on to the felt with two rows of running stitch (see page 7), using three strands of embroidery thread. Choose contrasting colours to the ribbon. Leaving 1cm (½in) between them, sew the remaining ribbons in place in the same way.

② Decorate the gaps between the ribbons with rows of running stitch using three strands of stranded cotton.

③ To make up the bag: pin the two other felt rectangles to the inside of the bag. Place two 30cm (12in) ribbons at the centre of each short end for the bag tie. Machine-stitch 5mm (¼in) from the edges in orange thread.

BELT★★

MATERIALS REQUIRED

7.5 x 90cm (3 x 35½in) red wool felt
1m (40in) ric-rac braid in turquoise
1m (40in) ric-rac braid in green
1m (40in) grosgrain 1.5cm (¾in) wide in green
1m (40in) grosgrain 8mm (³/₈in) wide in pink
1m (40in) grosgrain 8mm (³/₈in) wide in turquoise
1m (40in) cotton ribbon 1cm (½in) wide in pink
1m (40in) satin ribbon 5mm (¼in) wide in green
2 x 85cm (33½in) satin ribbon 5mm (¼in) wide in dark red
DMC stranded cotton in green, orange, turquoise, blue, pink
Needle
Orange thread
Eyelets and eyelet punch

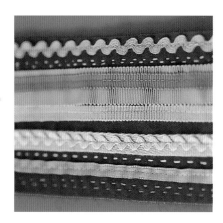

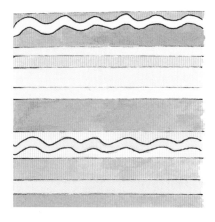

❶ Cut a strip of red felt approximately 90cm (35½in) long (to fit your hips) and 7.5cm (3in) wide. Start by machine-sewing the turquoise ric-rac along the upper edge of the belt using orange thread. Fold the ends of the ric-rac to the back of the felt.

❷ Add all the ribbons to the belt in this way, spacing them at roughly 5mm (¼in) intervals. The order is shown in the diagram. Sew the overlapping ribbons on one after the other.

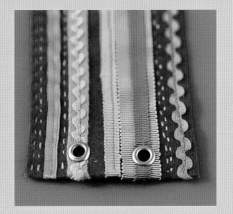 

3 Take three strands of stranded cotton and embroider rows of running stitch (see page 7) between the ribbons, using the picture from step 1 for inspiration.

4 Add two eyelets to each end of the belt. Using the eyelet punch, punch through the ribbon and the felt, place the eyelet in the hole and the other part on the back, and set the eyelet with the punch, following the instructions on page 62. Thread the satin ribbon through the eyelets to tie your belt.

ORGANZA STOLE ★★

*Organza and chiffon make perfect materials
for a stole for special occasions.*

MATERIALS REQUIRED

50cm x 2.25m (19¾ x 90in) red organza

1m (40in) of the following: silk ribbon 1cm (½in) wide in red and green, chiffon ribbon 5cm (2in) wide in green and dark red, thin red cord

50cm (19¾in) purple organza ribbon 3cm (1¼in) wide

Matching thread

Needle

1 dark red bead

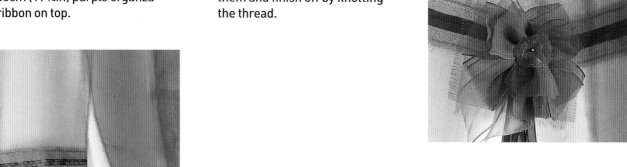

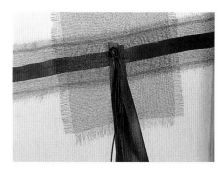

1 Cut one 2m x 50cm (80 x 19¾in) strip from the red organza for the stole, and two 50 x 5cm (19¾ x 2in) ribbons and one 12cm (4¾in) square.

2 Machine-sew one of the organza ribbons on to the end of the stole, with a 50cm (19¾in) green ribbon on top. Pin the second organza ribbon 20cm (8in) from the first with the red silk ribbon on top. Place the organza square 8cm (3¼in) from the side on top of the red silk ribbon. Sew on by machine. Sew a 50cm (19¾in) green chiffon ribbon 6cm (2½in) from the second ribbon, with a 50cm (19¾in) purple organza ribbon on top.

3 To make the flower, cut the dark red chiffon ribbon into six pieces of 6cm (2½in) and four pieces of 4cm (1⅝in). Cut two 6cm (2½in) lengths of green chiffon ribbon, cutting one of the ends at an angle. Assemble the 6cm (2½in) red and green ribbons and the 4cm (1⅝in) ribbons using a small running stitch (see page 7) and using the diagram as a guide. To make the flower shape, gather them and finish off by knotting the thread.

4 Cut out 3 discs of organza: one 3cm (1¼in) in diameter and two 2cm (⅞in) in diameter. Sew them into the centre of the flower with a bead. Sew a 44cm (17⅜in) red ribbon folded in half, 28cm (11in) green ribbon and two 50cm (19¾in) lengths of red cord folded in half to the centre of the square by machine. Sew the flower on to the ribbons.

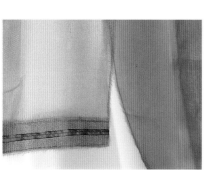

SPIRAL ART★★

*Thin ribbons rolled up to create a stunning
jewellery set with an ethnic flavour.*

MATERIALS REQUIRED **NECKLACE**

1.5m (60in) flat waxed cotton ribbon 4mm (¼in) wide in turquoise and khaki
and 50cm (19¾in) in yellow

Threads to match

Fine needle

Wooden skewer

❶ Make up five turquoise and
six khaki rolls. To make each
roll, cut a 30cm (12in) length
of ribbon. Thread a needle
with the same colour thread
as the ribbon. Wind the end
of the ribbon tightly around
the skewer, leaving 1cm (½in)
excess at the start.

❷ Thread your needle through
the double thickness ribbon,
then start to gradually wind
it around, securing it with
small stitches as you go. When
you have gone round three
times, remove the skewer and
continue to wind. Stop sewing
1cm (½in) from the end of the
ribbon, fold the end back and
secure the remaining length
with small stitches on the back
of the roll. Do the same for the
first excess length.

❸ Thread the turquoise and khaki
rolls on to a 50cm (19¾in)
length of yellow ribbon,
alternating the two colours.
Secure them as you go with
matching thread.

❹ For the clasp: make a small
2cm (⅞in) loop at one end of the
ribbon and secure with stitches
on the back. At the other end,
make a small roll from 25cm
(10in) turquoise ribbon for the
button and sew it on to the
yellow ribbon.

BRACELET★★

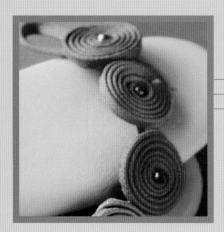

MATERIALS REQUIRED

50cm (19¾in) flat waxed cotton ribbon 4mm (¼in) wide in turquoise, khaki and blue, 1m (40in) in pink and 2m (80in) in orange
Small round beads in green and blue
Threads to match

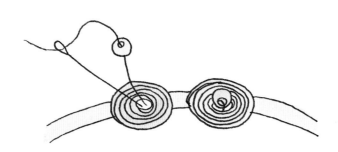

1 Using the same technique as the necklace on page 38, make up 10 small rolls of ribbon, using 25cm (10in) ribbon for each roll. Make three pink rolls, two blue rolls, two khaki rolls, two orange rolls and one green roll.

2 Attach the small rolls to the orange ribbon side by side with a bead sewn into the centre of each roll, using the diagram as a guide and alternating the colours of the beads as you go. Secure on the reverse with a couple of stitches once the bead is in place.

3 Fold the end of the orange ribbon back to form a 2cm (⁷⁄₈in) loop which you can hook around the first roll as a clasp.

PENDANT★★

MATERIALS REQUIRED

80cm (31½in) flat waxed cotton ribbon 4mm (¼in) wide in orange and 1m (40in) in pink

Roll up the orange ribbon as described for the necklace on page 38. Fold the pink ribbon in half and thread it into the centre, then thread the two ends through the loop and pull.

SHADES OF RIBBONS ★

Mix and match ribbons to add a delicate fringe to a necklace or scarf.

MATERIALS REQUIRED **NECKLACE**

1 thin metal choker

Offcuts or small lengths of ribbon in various shades of the same colour: satin ribbon, sheer ribbon, novelty ribbon, polyester ribbon, silk ribbon, velvet ribbon, and thin cord 5mm–1cm (¼–½in) wide

Make strips of ribbon 12cm (4¾in) long with the ends cut at an angle. To attach the ribbons to the metal necklace, fold in half and tie them around the circle, using diagrams A, B and C as a guide. Keep the ribbons knotted tightly against each other and cover the entire circle in this way.

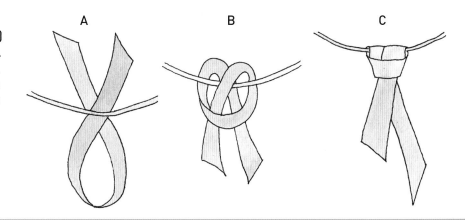

MATERIALS REQUIRED **SCARF**

14.5 x 92cm (5¾ x 36¼in) pink fleece

16 x 92cm (6½in x 36¼in) plum organza

50cm (20in) satin ribbon 1cm (½in) wide in red

Offcuts of ribbon as for necklace above

Matching thread

Needle

① Cut two 25cm (10in) lengths of satin ribbon. Cut 14cm (5½in) lengths of ribbon. Attach ribbon fringes to the two red ribbons using diagrams A, B and C as a guide. Keep the ribbons knotted tightly against each other until you have 15cm (6in) of fringe on each ribbon.

② Place the strip of fleece and the strip of organza on top of each other and pin them together. Place the fringe strips at each end of the scarf. Sew them on with small invisible stitches (see page 7) hidden in the knots in the ribbon fringe and joining the fleece and the organza at the same time.

WINTER SCARF★★

Wool and velvet ribbons make an elegant scarf for crisp winter days.

MATERIALS REQUIRED

50cm (20in) woollen fabric 150cm (60in) wide in light blue, brown and light green

1m (40in) velvet ribbon 1cm (½in) wide in dark red, khaki green, sky blue, brown and orange

Threads to match

Needle

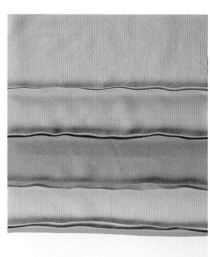

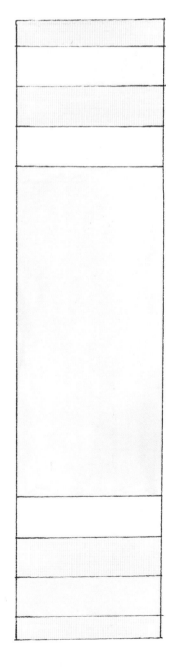

❷ The seams will be on the right side of the fabric. Press the seams open on the right side of the fabric. Cut 33cm (13in) lengths of ribbon, then sew them with a small blanket stitch on to the seams, tucking in 1cm (½in) at each end. Do not sew through the whole thickness of the scarf; leave the seams hanging free. Starting from one end of the scarf, alternate between ribbons in the following order: khaki, red, orange, brown, khaki, blue, brown, red.

❶ Cut the fabric as follows: Blue: 1 strip 76 x 31cm (30 x 12½in), 2 strips 13 x 31cm (5¼ x 12½in). Green: 2 strips 13 x 31cm (5¼ x 12½in). Brown: 2 strips 13 x 31cm (5¼ x 12½in), 2 strips 3 x 31cm (1¼ x 12½in). Join the strips wrong sides together 1.5cm (¾in) from the edges using the diagram as a guide to the order.

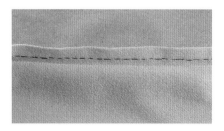

3 On the back of the scarf, iron your seams to flatten them out. Machine along the two long sides of the scarf, 5mm (¼in) from the edges, using light blue thread. Finish off at the level of the last ribbon to leave the end of the scarf open.

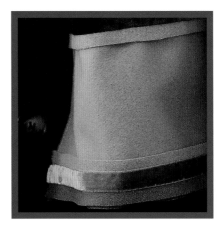

WOOLLEN NECK SCARF ★

MATERIALS REQUIRED

55 x 4cm (21¾ x 1⅝in) boiled wool in plum

1.10m (43½in) large multicolour fringing

40cm (15¾in) velvet ribbon 1cm (½in) wide in dark red

40cm (15¾in) velvet ribbon 1cm (½in) wide in chestnut brown

❶ Cut a 55 x 4cm (21¾ x 1⅝in) strip of wool. Cut the fringing in half. Sew a couple of blanket stitches across the end of the ribbon with a needle and thread to stop it from fraying.

❷ Sew the fringing along the two long edges of the strip of wool on the back of the scarf with small stitches.

❸ To finish off, sew a 40cm (15¾in) velvet ribbon on to the back of each end of the scarf. Cut the other ends of the ribbons at an angle to prevent fraying.

LACE CANDLEHOLDERS ★★★

These colourful candleholders create stunning effects when the candles are lit.

MATERIALS REQUIRED

3 cylindrical glasses

6 x 50cm (19¾in) lengths of fine lace ribbon in 6 different types

Wallpaper paste

Tissue paper in maroon, purple and pink

Coloured inks (red, purple, fuchsia)

Small foam roller

① Make up about half a bowlful of the wallpaper paste following the manufacturer's instructions for the water to powder ratio. Use a tape measure to measure the height and circumference of one of the glasses. Cut a strip of tissue paper the same size, adding 5mm (¼in) to the length of the circumference.

② With the tips of your fingers, coat the glass in a thin layer of glue, then place the strip of tissue paper on to the glue and wrap it around the glass, smoothing it out as you go. Leave to dry.

③ Place a strip of lace, the same length as the circumference of the glass, plus 5mm (¼in), on a protective sheet and dye it using the ink and your foam roller. Dye enough lengths of lace to cover the height of the glass. Hang the lace from some thread and leave to dry thoroughly, then iron.

④ Use your fingers to coat the lace in a little glue and lay it over the tissue paper, starting from the join in the paper. Leave to dry.

RIBBON WEAVE ★ ⌐

Different colours and materials are used to create this graphic effect.

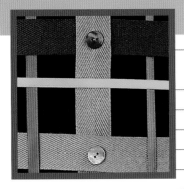

MATERIALS REQUIRED

1m x 50cm (40 x 20in) black corduroy

1m (40in) cotton ribbon 2.5cm (1in) wide in orange, red, grey, khaki and maroon

1m (40in) satin ribbon 5mm (¼in) wide in pink, orange, turquoise and khaki

Shell buttons 1.2cm (⅝in) in diameter, 6 green, 4 orange, 7 purple and 8 red

16 black buttons 1cm (½in) in diameter (optional)

Pins

Stuffing

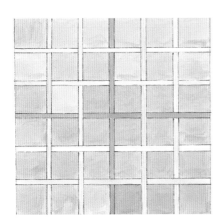

❶ Cut two 48cm (19in) squares from the black corduroy. Cut 48cm (19in) lengths of the cotton ribbons and pin them on to the cushion, using the diagram as a guide. Pin the satin ribbons between the cotton ribbons.

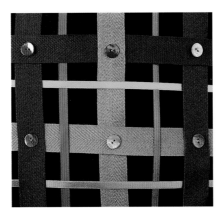

❷ Sew on shell buttons where the cotton ribbons cross to hold them in place. Sew the two sides of the cushion together, right sides together, leaving a 10cm (4in) opening. Turn the cushion right side out. Sew small black buttons on at the ends of the satin ribbons (optional).

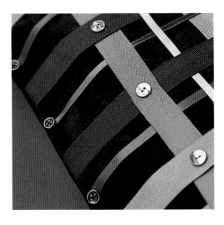

❸ Stuff the cushion through the opening, then sew up using ladder stitch (see page 7).

STORAGE BOX★★

*Strips of canvas, hessian and linen are woven together
to create this handy container with a 'recycled' theme.*

MATERIALS REQUIRED

55cm (21¾in) and 74cm (29¼in) lengths of assorted beige fabrics: ticking, heavy

linen, hessian and deckchair canvas

Beige sewing thread

Scissors

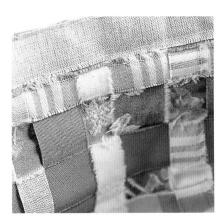

① Depending on the quality of the fabric, cut or tear the different fabrics to make six 55 x 2cm (21¾ x ⁷⁄₈in) ribbons, eight 55 x 3cm (21¾ x 1¼in) ribbons, four 74 x 3cm (29¼ x 1¼in) ribbons and two 74 x 2cm (29¼ x ⁷⁄₈in) ribbons. Lay seven 55cm (21¾in) ribbons out flat in front of you, vertically side by side. Weave the seven other 55cm (21¾in) ribbons horizontally through the first series of ribbons and pin as you go, using the diagram as a guide. Sew a square around the base to secure.

② On one side of the box, along the base, lay one 74cm (29¼in) ribbon at one corner and pin. Weave horizontally. At the next corner, turn and weave the ribbon along the side of the box. Continue along the four sides. Weave in the different 74cm (29¼in) ribbons as you work upwards to give you a square box. Pin as you work.

③ Along the upper edge, fold the ends of the ribbons over to the inside of the container. Pin. Cut a heavy linen ribbon 74 x 3cm (29¼ x 1¼in) and machine-sew it around the inside top edge of the container, along both the edges of the ribbon.

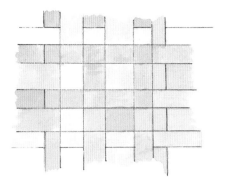

ORGANZA HANGING★★★

Pastel shades make a delicate window hanging.

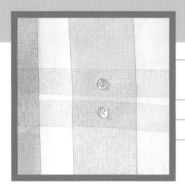

MATERIALS REQUIRED

White organza to fit your window, plus 1cm (½in) all round for the hem

Sheer ribbon 2cm (⁷/₈in), 2.5cm (1in), 3cm (1¼in), 4cm (1⁵/₈in), 5cm (2in), 8cm (3¼in) wide in the colours of your choice

62 small shell buttons (depending on the size of your curtain)

White thread

① Make a 5mm (¼in) double hem all the way around your panel. Pin and machine-sew. Cut nine ribbons of different colours and thicknesses the same length as your panel, and eleven ribbons of different colours and thicknesses the same width as your panel.

② Pin two ribbons lengthways on to your panel 1.5cm (¾in) from the two outer edges, then spread the other ribbons out evenly between them, using diagram A for inspiration. Pin to secure.

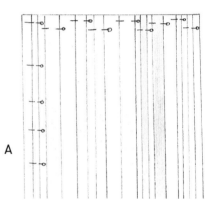

A

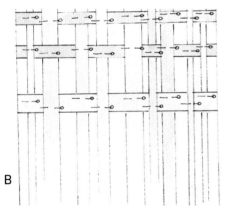

B

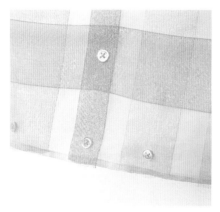

③ Weave the horizontal ribbons between the vertical ribbons and secure at each join with a pin (diagram B).

④ At each end of the vertical and horizontal ribbons, sew on a small shell button. According to the number of joins you have, sew on the shell buttons evenly over the curtain to secure the ribbons. Use the picture for inspiration.

PATCHWORK OF RIBBONS ★

A collage of ribbons to frame a special memory.

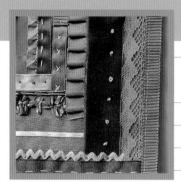

MATERIALS REQUIRED

30cm (12in) square of orange satin

112cm (43⅞in) grosgrain ribbon 1cm (½in) wide in green and offcuts of orange and green ribbons

DMC stranded cotton in orange and green

30cm (12in) square of iron-on fabric

Dressmaker's pencil

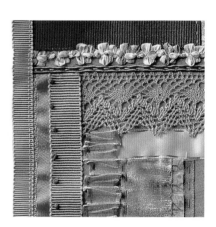

① Iron the iron-on fabric on to the reverse of the 30cm (12in) square of orange satin. Using a dressmaker's pencil, draw a 28cm (11in) square and then a 10cm (4in) square inside it.

② Sew the 1cm (½in) wide grosgrain ribbon all the way around, 1cm (½in) from the edge of the orange satin. Sew on the ribbon offcuts working around the frame and using the picture for inspiration. Make sure the ends overlap so that they do not fray. Attach the ribbons with a running stitch, cross stitch or French knots (see page 7) using three strands of orange or green stranded cotton. Vary the length of the stitches. Trim any excess orange satin close to the green grosgrain.

③ To hang the frame up, sew two small loops along the top edge using some grosgrain.

SUMMER THROW ★★★

Linen and ribbons work together in this very trendy throw!

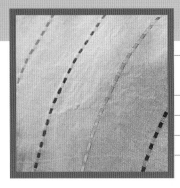

MATERIALS REQUIRED

1.5m (60in) square of raw linen

3m (120in) satin ribbon 7mm (¼in) wide in orange, turquoise, dark red, lime green and brick red

Embroidery scissors

Dressmaker's pencil

Pin

 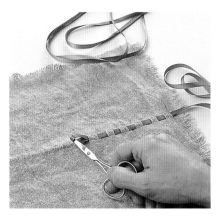 

❶ Start by washing the linen as it is liable to shrink. Cut a 1.34m (52¾in) square piece. Make a 1cm (½in) fringe all the way around the outside of the fabric. Make a mark every 12cm (4¾in) along one edge with a dressmaker's pencil. Using the points of your embroidery scissors, pull out threads across the fabric over about an 8mm (³/₈in) width.

❷ Weave the satin ribbons through the pulled threads at intervals of approximately 1cm (½in). Alternate the colours as follows: brick red, lime green, dark red, turquoise, orange. Leave about 1.5cm (¾in) excess ribbon at each end.

❸ With the ribbons flat on the table fringe the ends using a pin. Machine-stitch all the way around to secure the fringing and stop the ribbons from sliding out.

FLORAL LIGHT ★

Ends of tulle, satin and silk, and a little mesh,
make a lovely table decoration and soft lighting.

MATERIALS REQUIRED

2m (80in) satin, silk and sheer blue and turquoise ribbons 3mm–1.5cm (⅛–¾in) wide

1m (40in) turquoise tulle netting

1m (40in) of 1cm (½in) wide silk ribbon in light green, sheer ribbon in light green and sheer ribbon in turquoise

17 x 9cm (6¾ x 3½in) wire mesh with 5mm (¼in) squares

Thin wire

1 circle of foam board 5cm (2in) in diameter

1 refrigerator lightbulb and 3m (120in) electrical cable

1 screw socket

Acrylic paint in almond green and turquoise and glass paint in blue

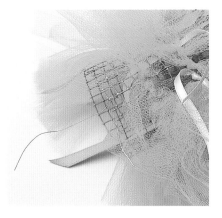

① For the first row of the lampshade, cut out 13 ribbons 28 x 8cm (11 x 3¼in) from tulle netting. Cut 23cm (9in) lengths from your satin ribbons (you will need around 18). Cut the ends at an angle to prevent fraying. For the second row, cut 13 ribbons 20 x 8cm (8 x 3¼in) from tulle netting and 20cm (8in) lengths of the other ribbons. For the last row, cut 13 ribbons 15 x 6cm (6 x 2½in) from tulle netting.

② Knot the ribbons to the edge of the mesh. Alternate between tulle ribbons and cut ribbons. Tie the second row 4cm (1⅝in) from the first and the last 3cm (1¼in) from the second. Bend the mesh into a cylinder and secure with thin twisted wire. Trim the excess.

③ Using acrylic paint, paint the circle of foam board turquoise and the electric cable in almond green. Paint the lightbulb blue using glass paint. Make a hole in the centre of the foam board and put the socket together.

④ Cut 16cm (6½in) lengths of green and turquoise ribbon and tie them in threes along the electric cable, spacing them approximately every 13cm (5¼in).

MULTICOLOUR
MEMO BOARD ★★★

Use this fun stripy memo board to store notes and cards.

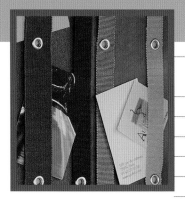

MATERIALS REQUIRED

1 wooden frame (inside measurement 46cm (18in) square)

1m (40in) grosgrain ribbon 1.5cm (¾in) wide in turquoise, green, yellow and plum and 2.5cm (1in) wide in orange

46 x 12cm (18 x 5in) felt in red, brown, orange, green and blue

Acrylic paint in turquoise blue

Eyelet punch and setting device

Small gold eyelets 1cm (½in) in diameter

Ribbon fabric glue and white PVA glue

Dressmaker's pencil

1 large paintbrush

1 piece stiff card 46cm (18in) square

① Cut out the following in your felt:
red 46 x 11cm (18 x 4³/₈in)
brown 46 x 8cm (18 x 3¼in)
orange 46 x 5cm (18 x 2in)
khaki 46 x 12cm (18 x 4¾in)
blue 46 x 10cm (18 x 4in).
Then cut two pieces 50cm (19¾in) long in each colour ribbon.

② Pin the ribbons on to the strips of felt, using the diagram of the ribbon layout on page 64 as a guide. Leave 1cm (½in) excess ribbon at each end.

③ Make a mark with the pencil 6cm (2½in) or 12cm (4¾in) from each end of the ribbon and in the centre. Refer to the diagram on page 64 for the positions of the eyelets on each ribbon. Using the punch, make a hole through the ribbon and the felt, place the eyelet in the hole and the other part on the back, and set the eyelet with the setting tool. Repeat for each strip.

④ Fold the ends of the ribbons over and glue them on to the reverse of the felt with fabric glue. Using a brush, paint the card with PVA glue and carefully stick on the strips of felt side by side. Paint the frame in a colour to match one of the ribbons and place your design in the frame.

TEMPLATES

Multicolour memo board (page 62)

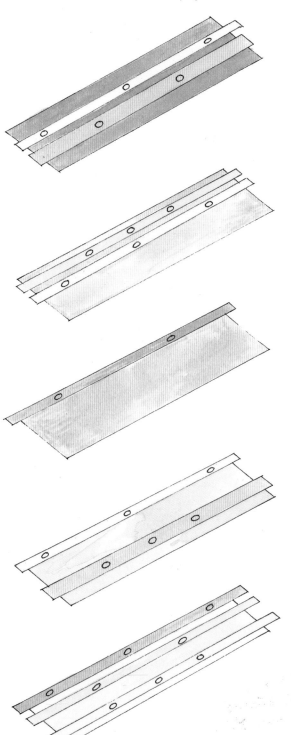

Customized jeans (page 28)

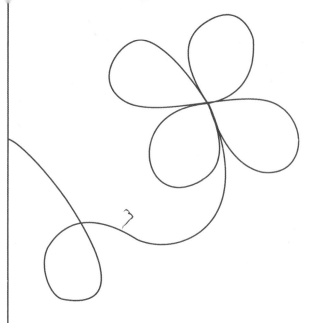